PHONICS
Workbook

MOONSTONE

Published in Moonstone
by Rupa Publications India Pvt. Ltd 2022
7/16, Ansari Road, Daryaganj
New Delhi 110002

Sales centres:
Allahabad Bengaluru Chennai
Hyderabad Jaipur Kathmandu
Kolkata Mumbai

P-ISBN: 978-93-5520-648-0
E-ISBN: 978-93-5520-649-7

First impression 2022

10 9 8 7 6 5 4 3 2 1

Contents

Trace and Learn

Trace the lines.

Sleeping lines

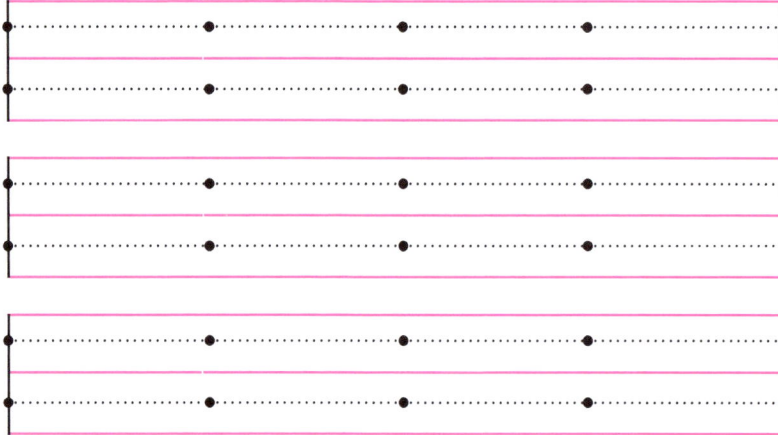

Standing lines

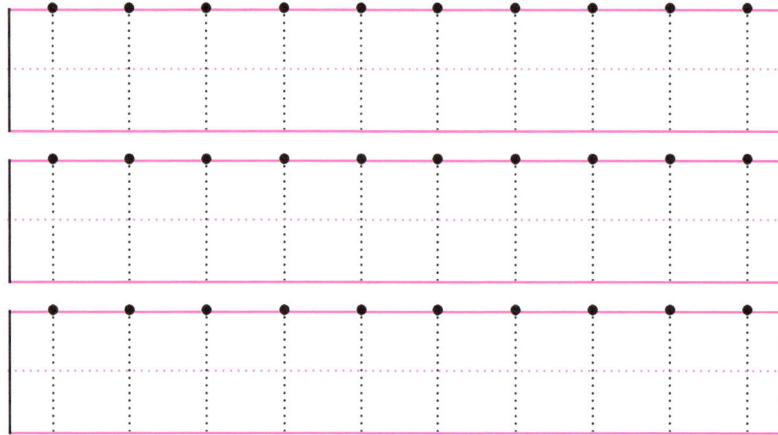

Slanting lines

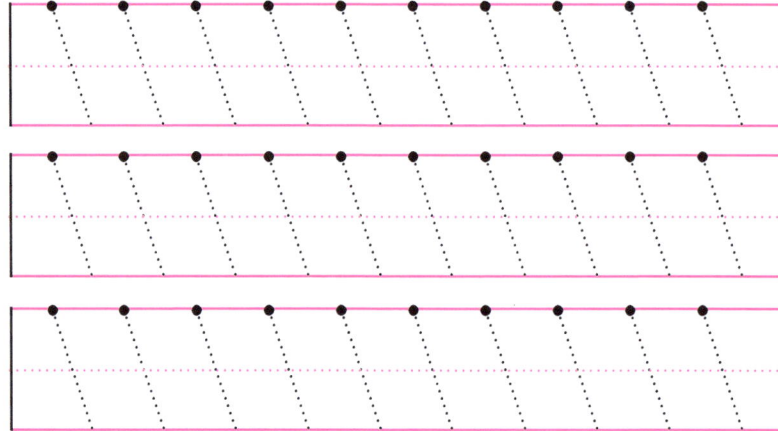

Teaching Tips: First, teach the child the tripod grip. Teach sleeping lines as if a body is resting on a bed, how we sleep on a bed; standing lines as a tall tree stands and slanting lines by drawing raindrops.

Slanting lines

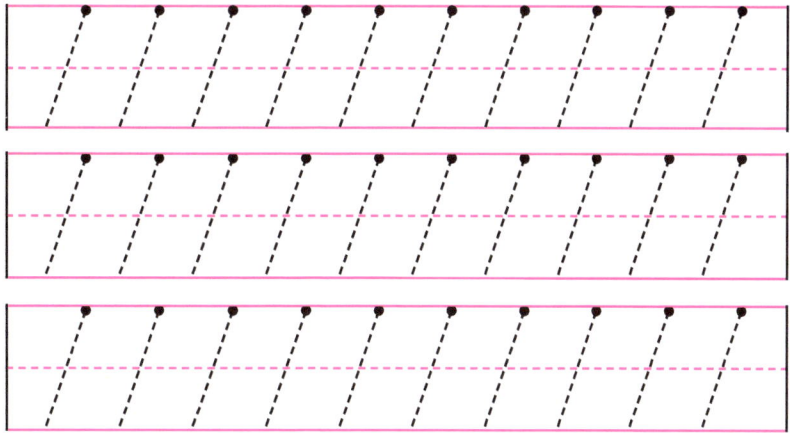

Curved lines

 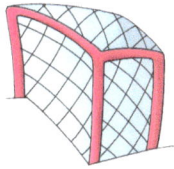 

Zig Zag lines

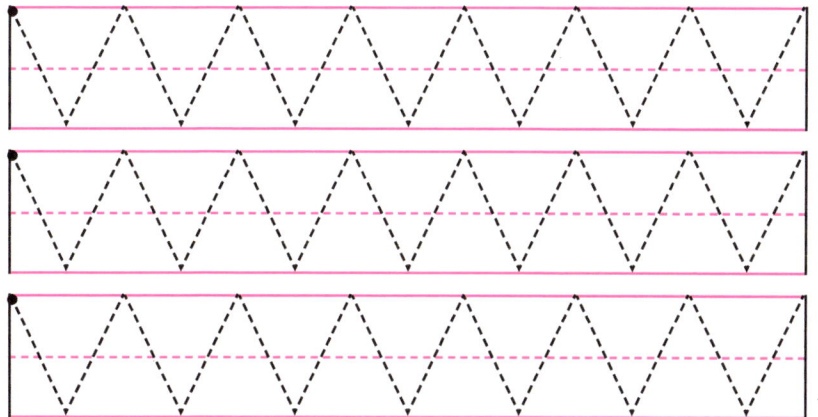

Teaching Tips: Focus on the tripod grip. Teach c by drawing the shape in the air. Teach the children to write v and w in the air.

A a

Write the letter a in the air. Write a with your finger on the table. Say the sound: a-a-a.

Trace and colour the picture.

Trace the letters A and a.

Say the names of these objects.

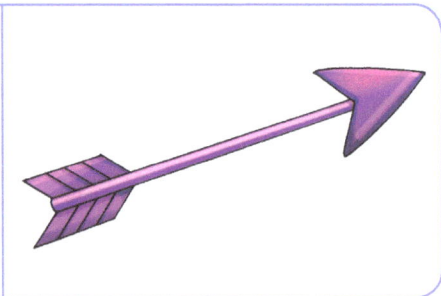

6

B b

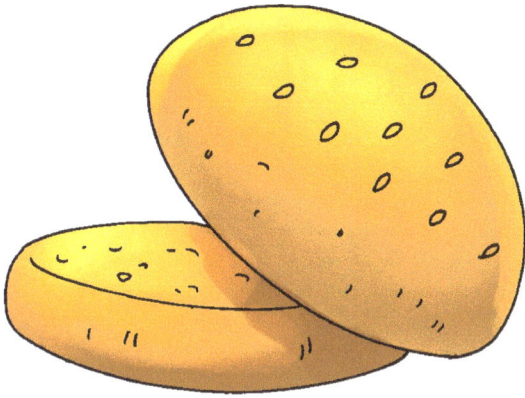

Write the letter b in the air. Write b with your finger on the table. Say the sound: b-b-b.

Trace and colour the picture.

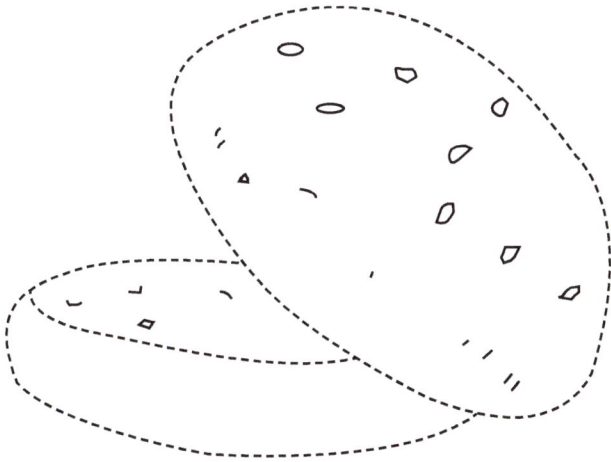

Trace the letters B and b.

Say the names of these objects.

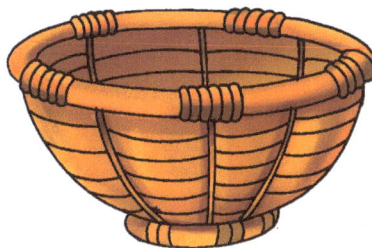

7

Fun with A and B

Circle the objects that start with an a.

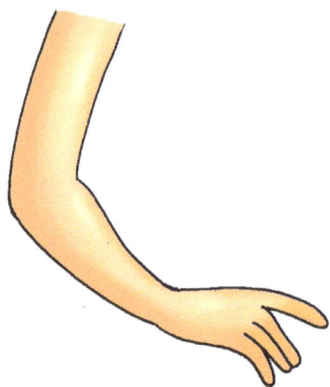

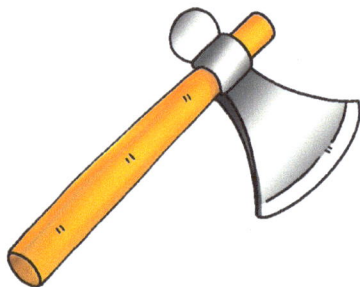

Trace the dotted lines to complete the butterflies.

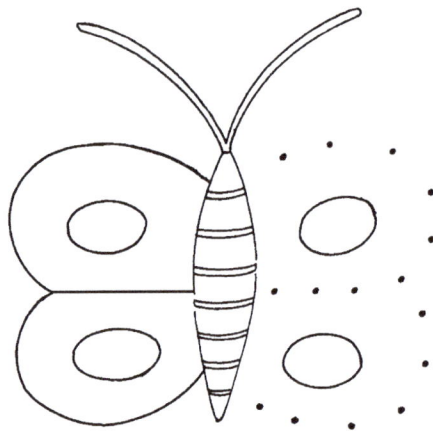

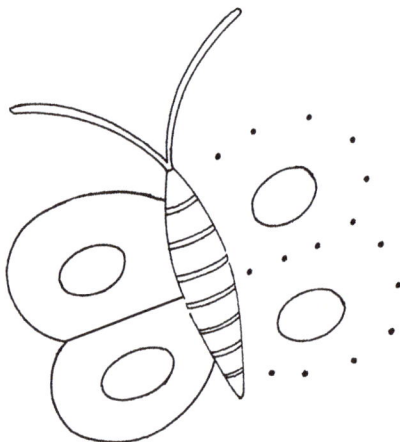

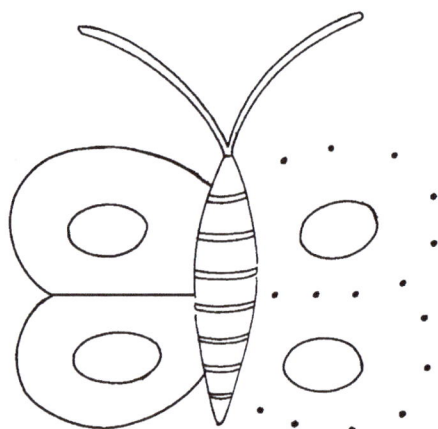

C c

Write the letter c in the air. Write c with your finger on the table. Say the sound: c-c-c.

Trace and colour the picture.

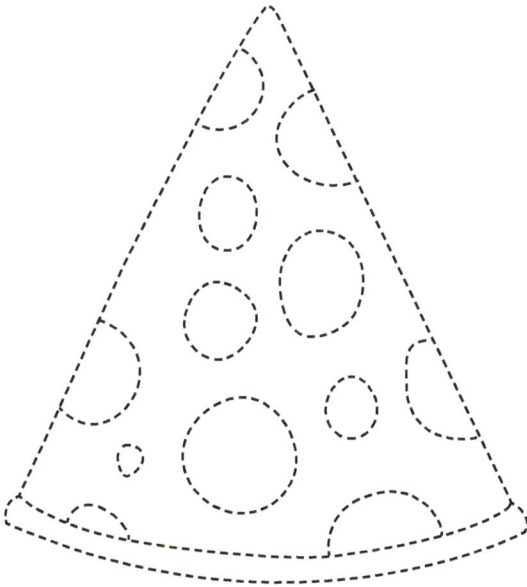

Trace the letters C and c.

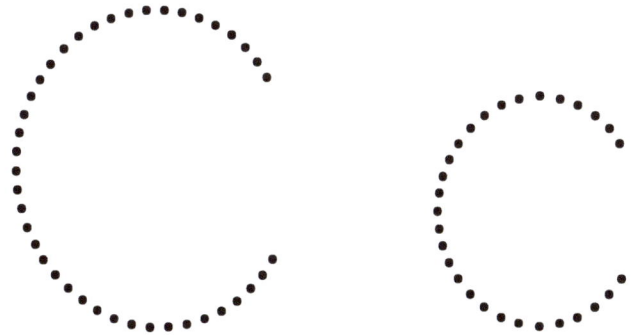

Say the names of these objects.

D d

Write the letter d in the air. Write d with your finger on the table. Say the sound: d-d-d.

Trace and colour the picture.

Trace the letters D and d.

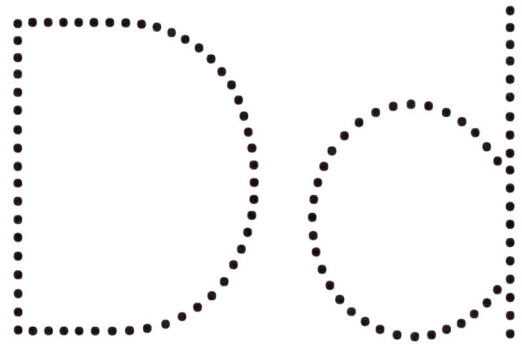

Say the names of these objects.

Fun with C and D

Colour the animals that start with d.

Complete the words.

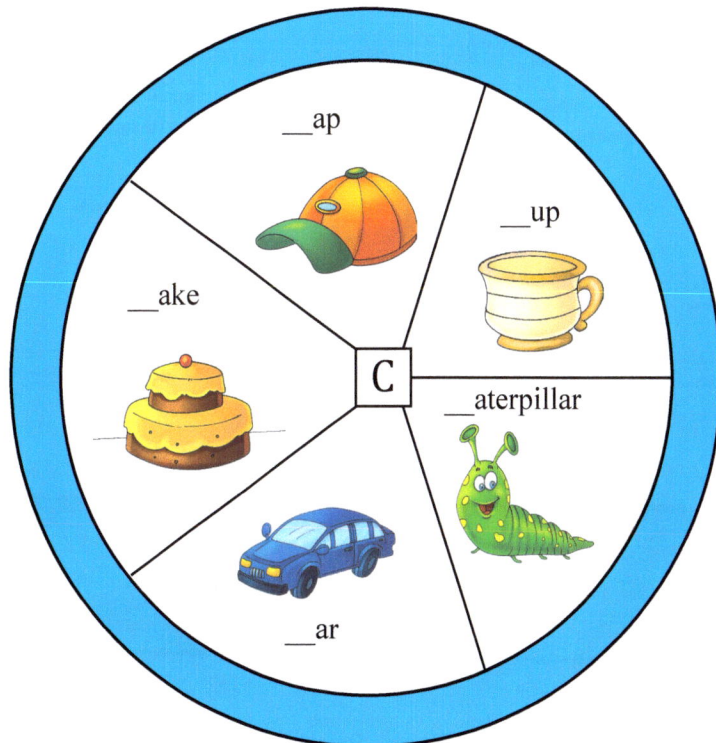

__ap

__up

__ake

__aterpillar

C

__ar

E e

Write the letter e in the air. Write e with your finger on the table. Say the sound: e-e-e.

Trace and colour the picture.

Trace the letters E and e.

Say the names of these objects.

F f

Write the letter f in the air. Write f with your finger on the table. Say the sound: f-f-f.

Trace and colour the picture.

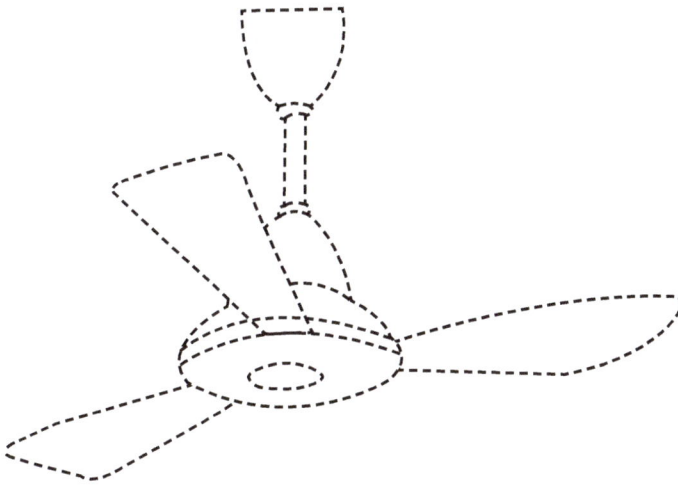

Trace the letters F and f.

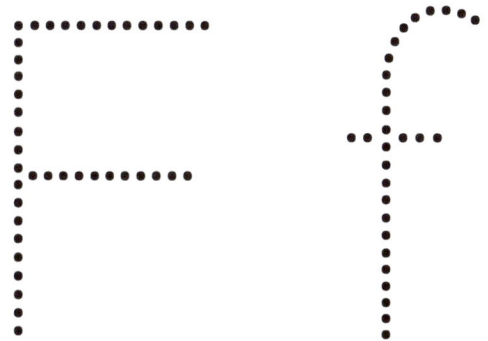

Say the names of these objects.

 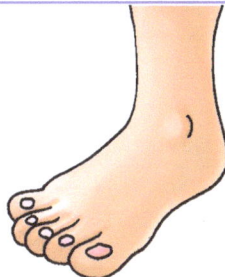 

Fun with E and F

Can you find the following words in the word search below?

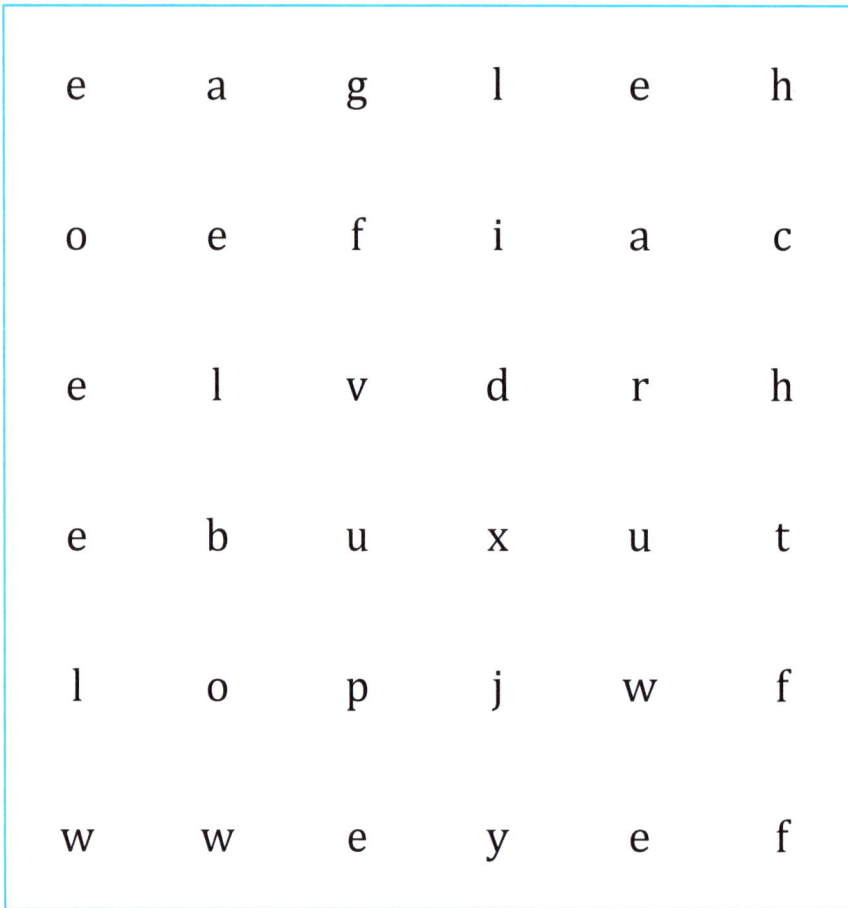

e	a	g	l	e	h
o	e	f	i	a	c
e	l	v	d	r	h
e	b	u	x	u	t
l	o	p	j	w	f
w	w	e	y	e	f

ear

eye

eagle

eel

elbow

Circle the objects that begin with the f sound.

G g

Write the letter g in the air. Write g with your finger on the table. Say the sound: g-g-g.

Trace and colour the picture.

Trace the letters G and g.

Say the names of these objects.

  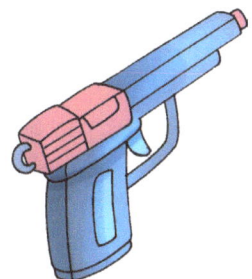

H h

Write the letter h in the air. Write h with your finger on the table. Say the sound: h-h-h.

Trace and colour the picture.

Trace the letters H and h.

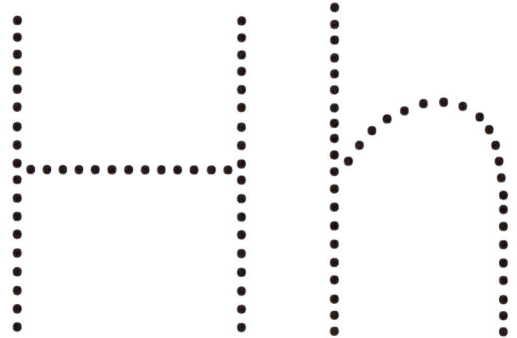

Say the names of these objects.

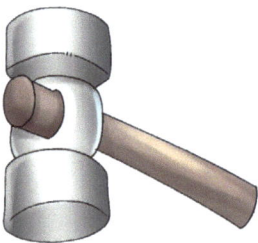

Fun with G and H

Colour the objects that begin with the g sound.

Colour the house.

I i

Write the letter i in the air. Write i with your finger on the table. Say the sound: i-i-i.

Trace and colour the picture.

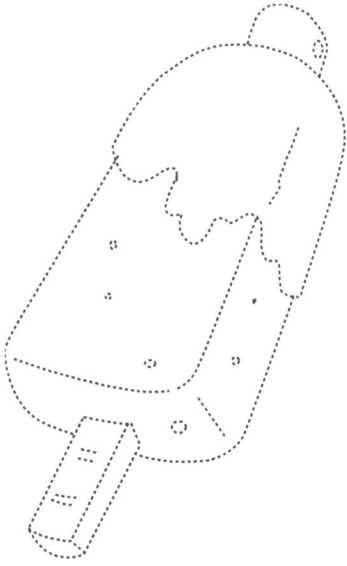

Trace the letters I and i.

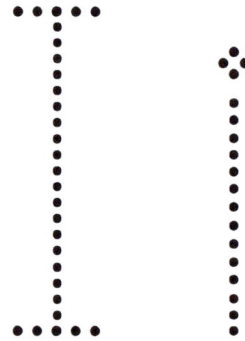

Say the names of these objects.

18

J j

Write the letter j in the air. Write j with your finger on the table. Say the sound: j-j-j.

Trace and colour the picture.

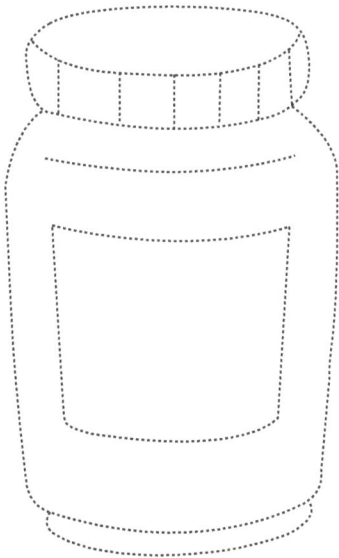

Trace the letters J and j.

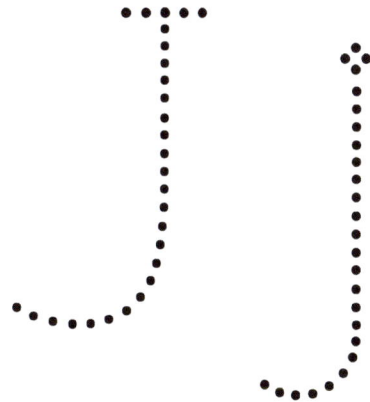

Say the names of these objects.

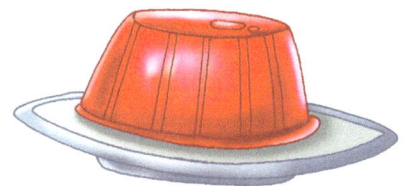

Fun with I and J

Draw and colour an ice cream.

Trace and colour the joker.

Teaching Tips: Ask the children to draw other objects that begin with an 'i' sound. For example, ice-cube, igloo, etc.

20

K k

k as in kite

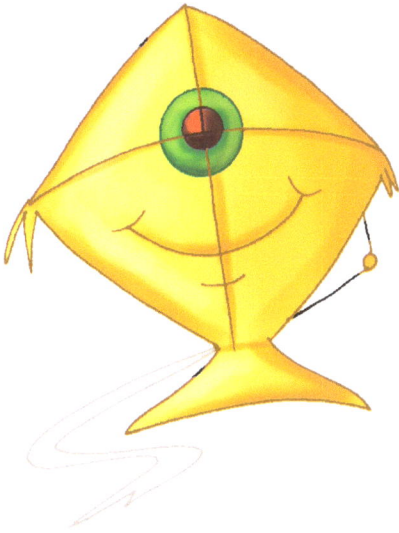

Write the letter k in the air. Write k with your finger on the table. Say the sound: k-k-k.

Trace and colour the picture.

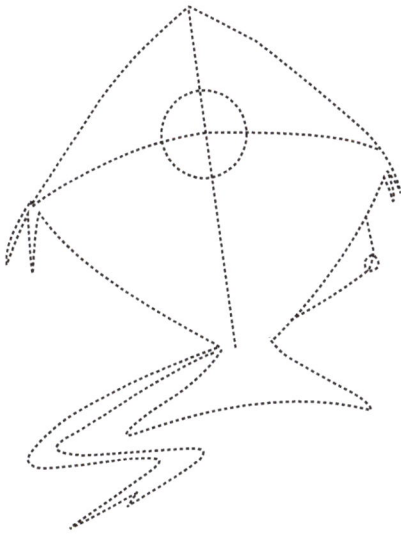

Trace the letters K and k.

Say the names of these objects.

L l

l as in leaf

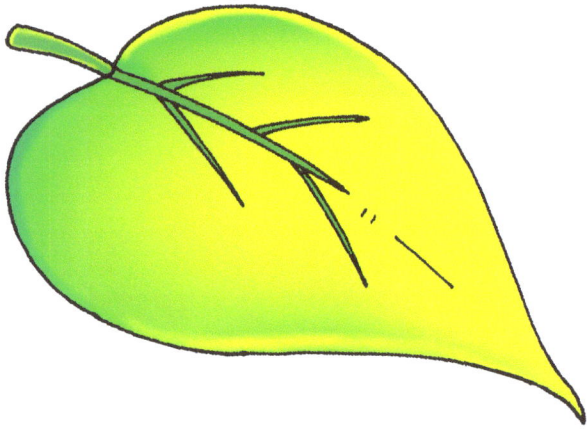

Write the letter l in the air. Write l with your finger on the table. Say the sound: l-l-l.

Trace and colour the picture.

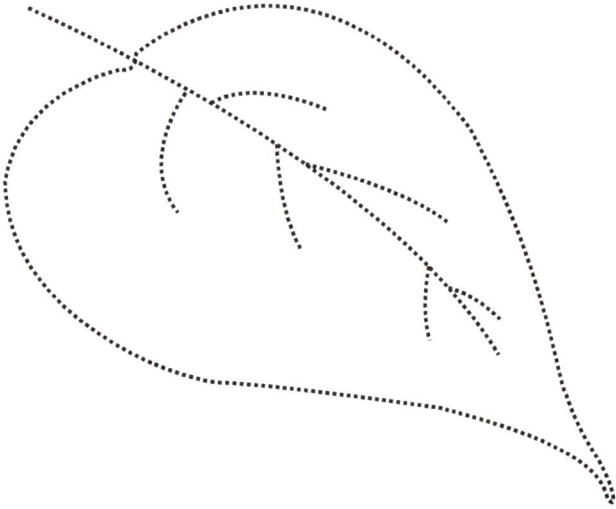

Trace the letters L and l.

Say the names of these objects.

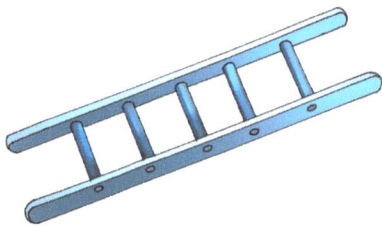

Fun with K and L

Join the letters from A to K to complete the kitten.

A

K • • B

• C • D

J •

• E

I •

• F

H • • G

Write L and l on the ladybugs.

M m

m as in moon

Write the letter m in the air. Write m with your finger on the table. Say the sound: m-m-m.

Trace and colour the picture.

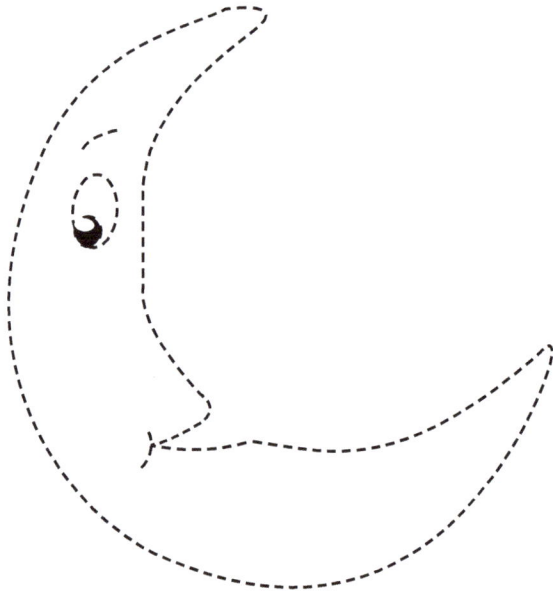

Trace the letters M and m.

Say the names of these objects.

N n

Write the letter n in the air. Write n with your finger on the table. Say the sound: n-n-n.

Trace and colour the picture.

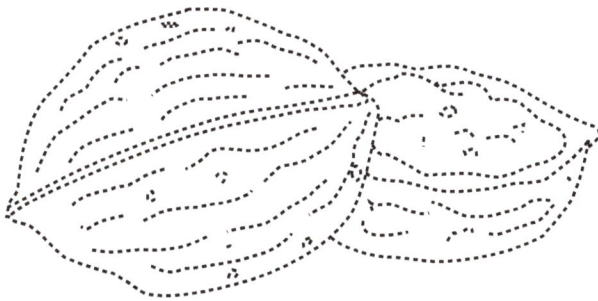

Trace the letters N and n.

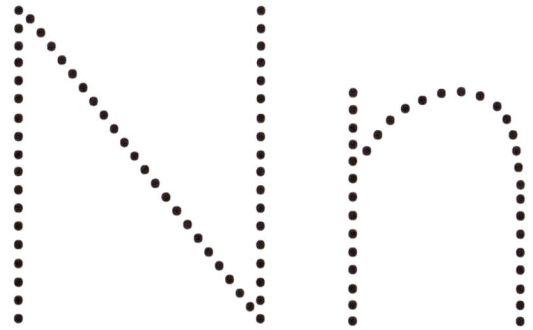

Say the names of these objects.

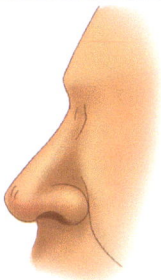

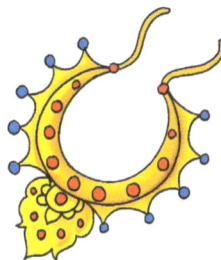

25

Fun with M and N

Colour the mountains brown.

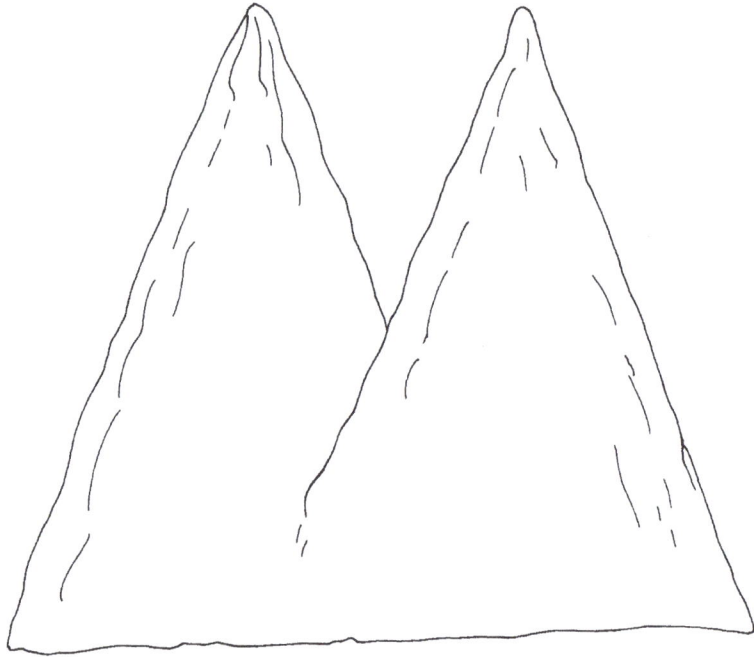

Draw two eggs in the nest.

O o

Write the letter o in the air. Write o with your finger on the table. Say the sound: o-o-o.

Trace and colour the picture.

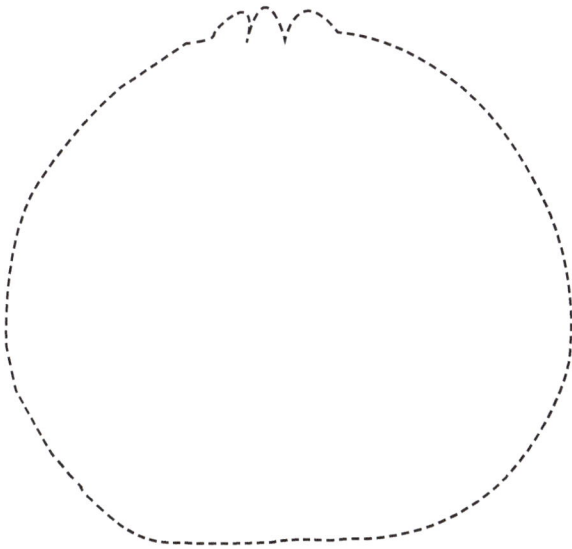

Trace the letters O and o.

Say the names of these objects.

P p

p as in pan

Write the letter p in the air. Write p with your finger on the table. Say the sound: p-p-p.

Trace and colour the picture.

Trace the letters P and p.

Say the names of these objects.

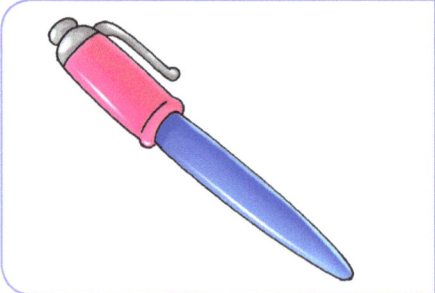

Fun with O and P

Trace and colour the octopus.

Colour the cake pink and draw candles on it.

Q q

q as in queen

Write the letter q in the air. Write q with your finger on the table. Say the sound: q-q-q.

Trace and colour the picture.

Trace the letters Q and q.

Say the names of these objects.

R r

Write the letter r in the air. Write r with your finger on the table. Say the sound: r-r-r.

Trace and colour the picture.

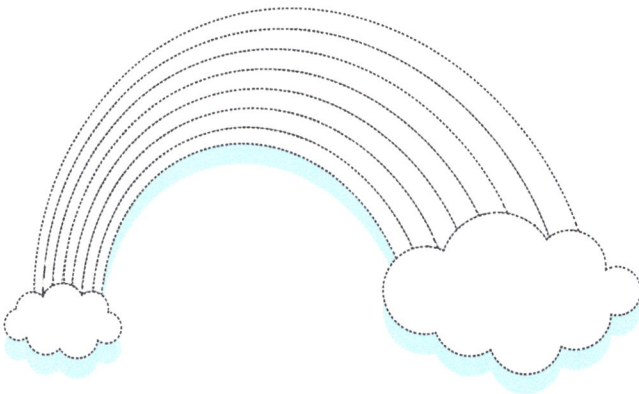

Trace the letters R and r.

Say the names of these objects.

31

Fun with Q and R

Find the **q**s in the question mark.

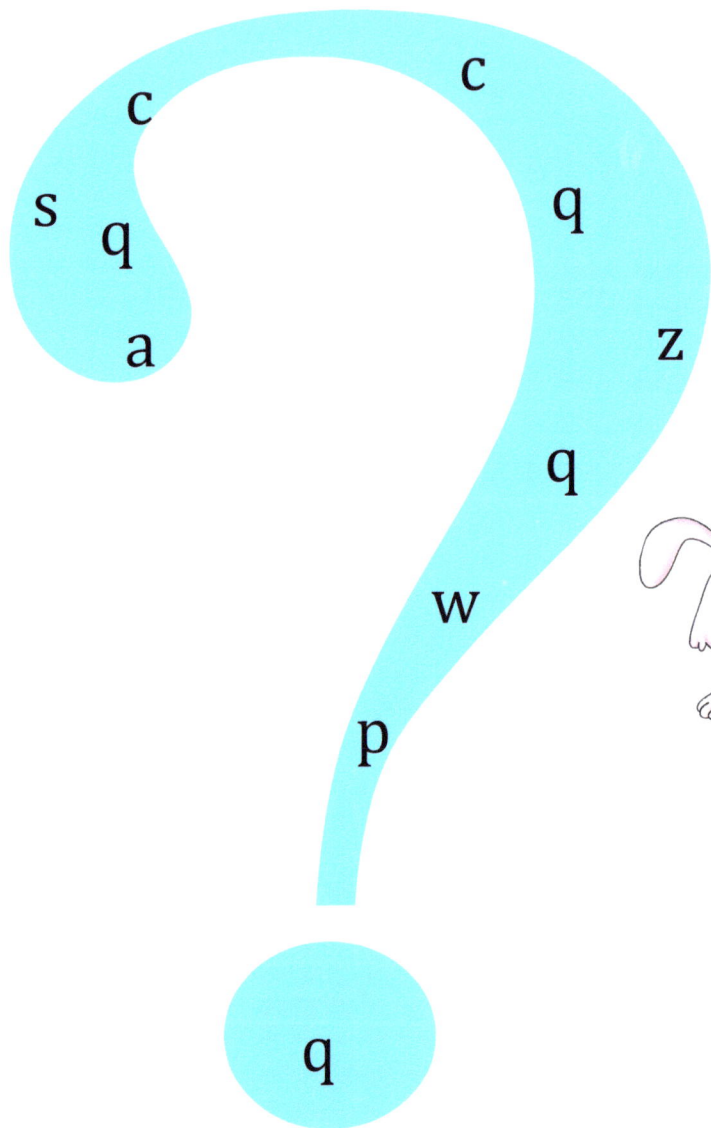

c

s

c

q

q

a

z

q

Help the rabbit find its way to the carrots.

w

p

q

S s

Write the letter s in the air. Write s with your finger on the table. Say the sound: s-s-s.

Trace and colour the picture.

Trace the letters S and s.

Say the names of these objects.

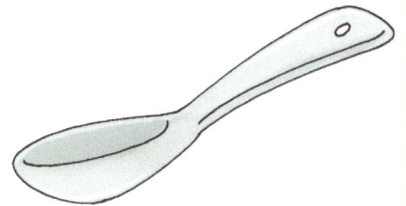

T t

Write the letter t in the air. Write t with your finger on the table. Say the sound: t-t-t.

Trace and colour the picture.

Trace the letters T and t.

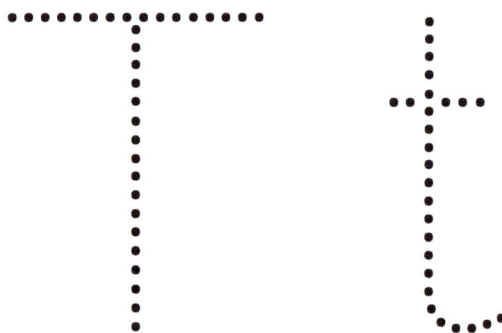

Say the names of these objects.

34

Fun with S and T

Help the snake reach the snail.

Join the dots to complete the turkey.

U u

Write the letter u in the air. Write u with your finger on the table. Say the sound: u-u-u.

Trace and colour the picture.

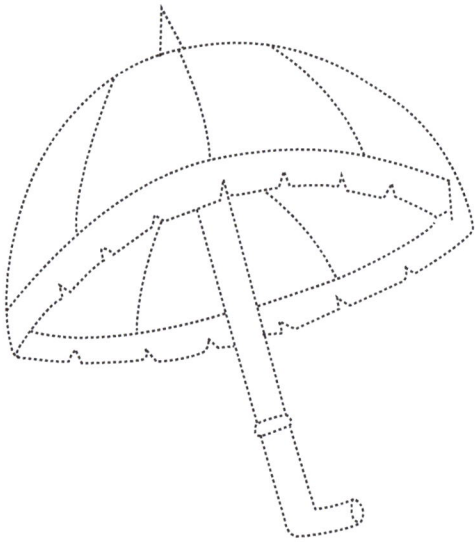

Trace the letters U and u.

Say the names of these objects.

V v

Write the letter v in the air. Write v with your finger on the table. Say the sound: v-v-v.

Trace and colour the picture.

Trace the letters V and v.

Say the names of these objects.

Fun with U and V

Join the dots from a to u and colour the picture.

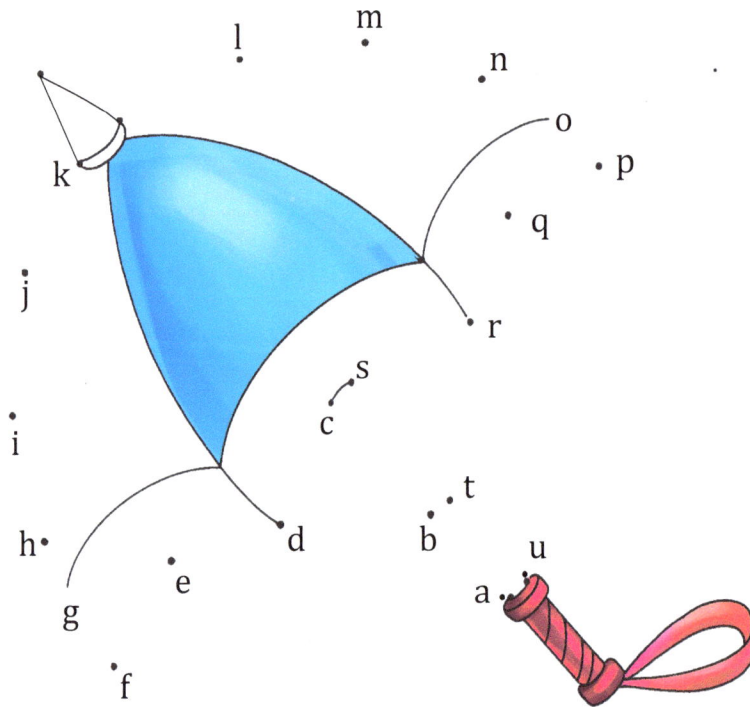

Draw a few flowers in the vase and colour the picture.

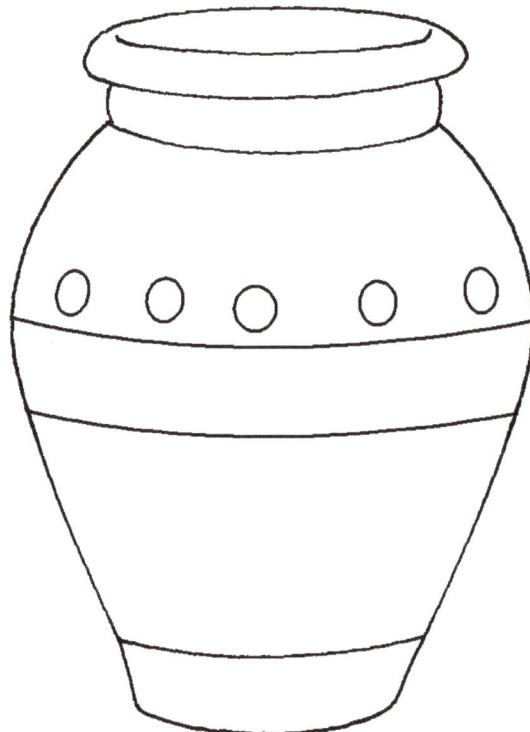

W w

w as in well

Write the letter w in the air. Write w with your finger on the table. Say the sound: w-w-w.

Trace and colour the picture.

Trace the letters W and w.

Say the names of these objects.

X x

Write the letter x in the air. Write x with your finger on the table. Say the sound: x-x-x.

Trace and colour the picture.

Trace the letters X and x.

X x

Say the names of these objects.

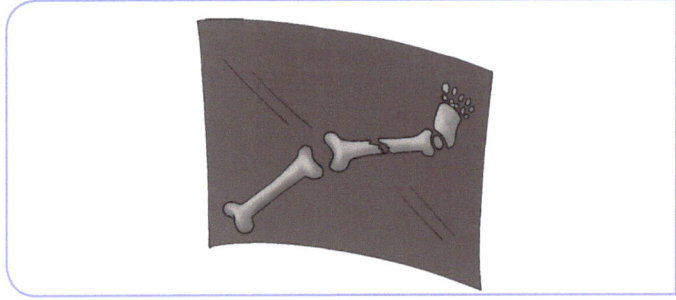

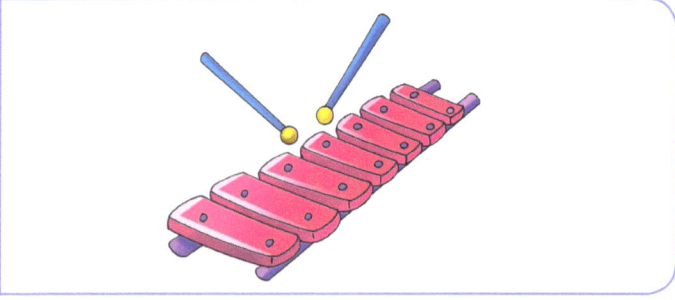

Fun with W and X

Connect the objects that begin with the w sound to the W at the centre.

W

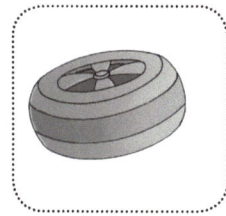

Colour the xylophone with different colours.

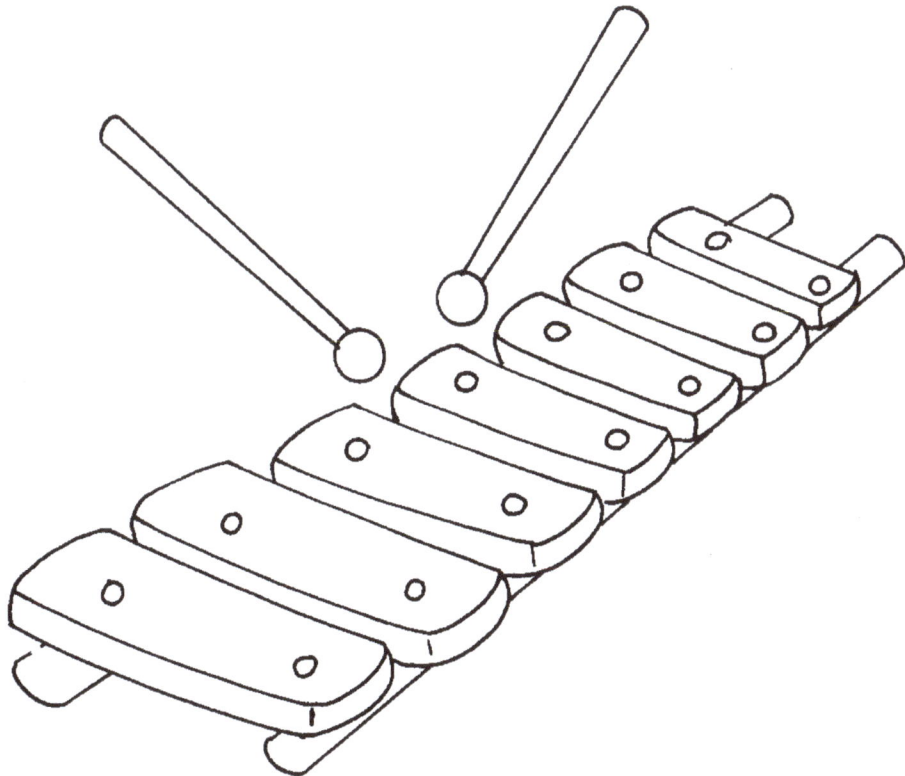

Y y

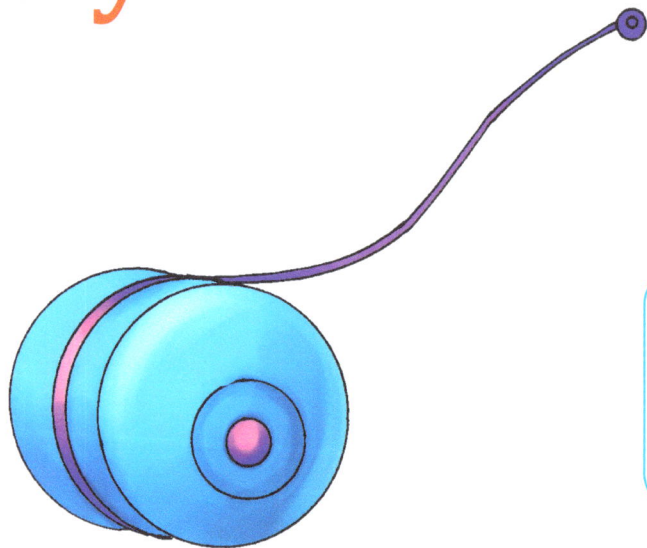

y as in yo-yo

Write the letter y in the air. Write y with your finger on the table. Say the sound: y-y-y.

Trace and colour the picture.

Trace the letter Y and y.

Say the names of these objects.

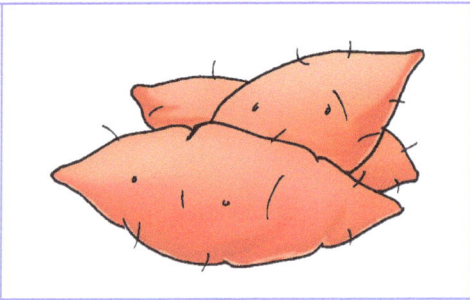

Z z

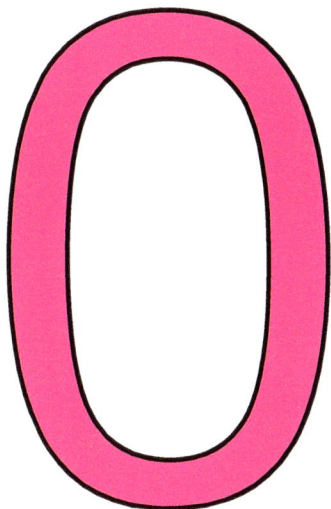

Write the letter z in the air. Write z with your finger on the table. Say the sound: z-z-z.

Trace and colour the picture.

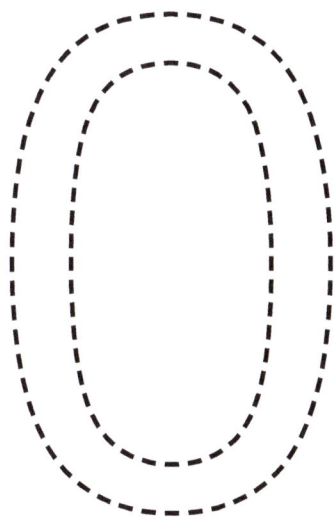

Trace the letter Z and z.

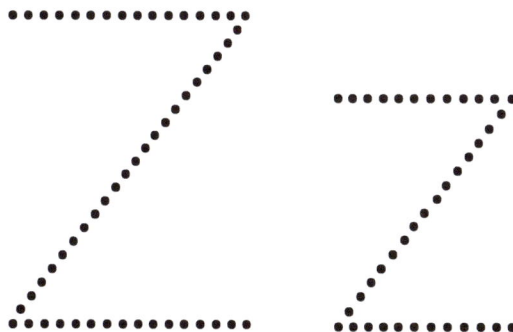

Say the names of these objects.

Fun with Y and Z

Draw the horns, the eyes and the nose to turn the Y into a yak.

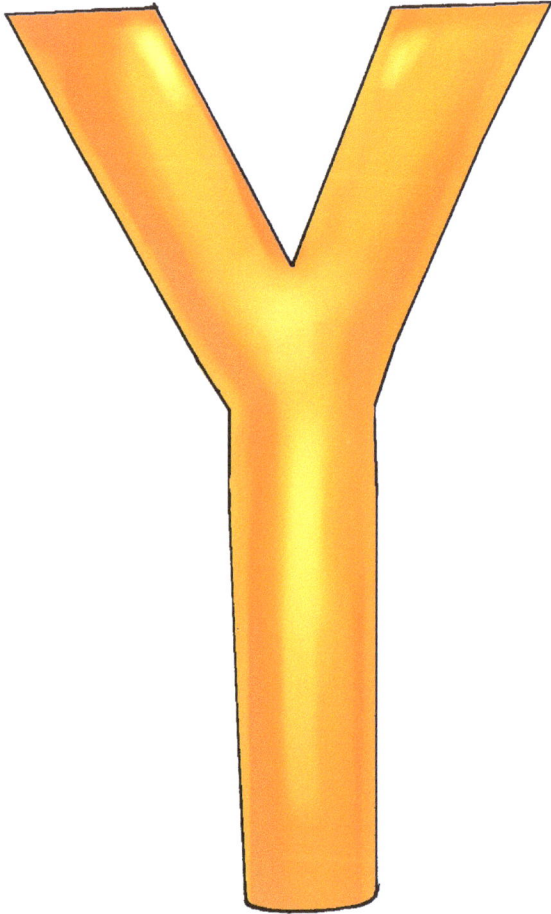

Help the zebra find its way to the zoo.

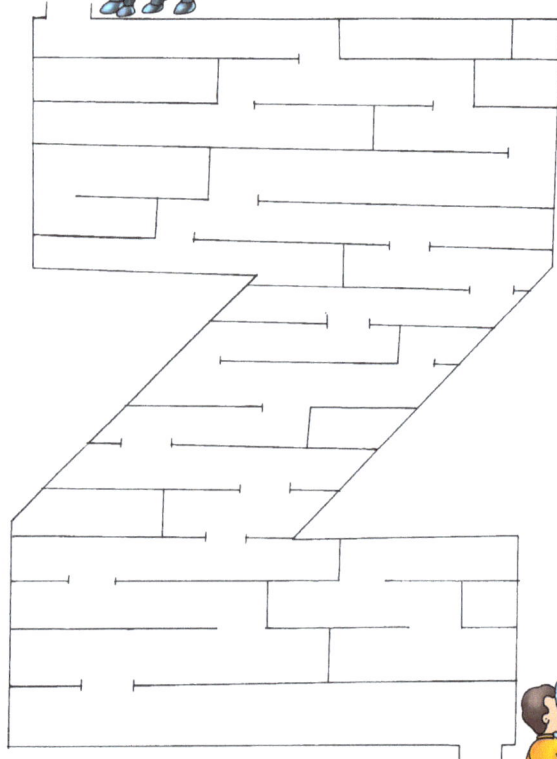

Let's Revise-1

It is raining letters. Fill the rain droplets with the missing letters.

A   ___   C   ___   E

F   ___   H   ___   J

K   ___   M   ___   O

P   ___   R   ___   T

U   ___   W   ___   Y

Z

Let's Revise-2

Fill in the letters a-z in the caterpillar's body.

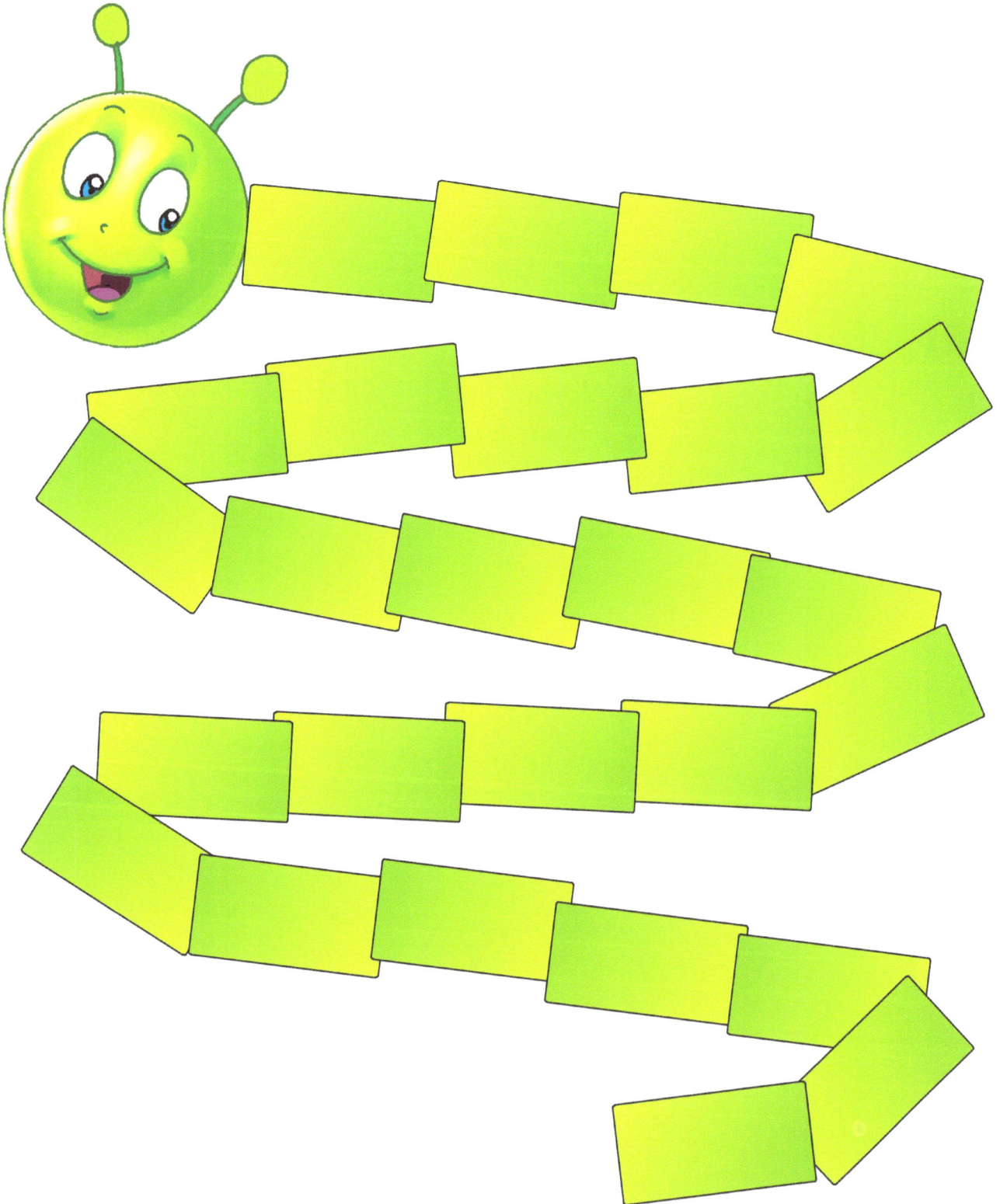

Find the Path

Help the duckling reach mother duck by following the path of the letters from **A** to **Z**.

Start

A   B

C

D

E   F

G

H

I

J

K

L

M

N

O

P   Q

R

S   T

U

V   W

X

Y

Z

Finish

Matching Fun

Match the correct uppercase and lowercase letters.

www.ingramcontent.com/pod-product-compliance
Lightning Source LLC
Chambersburg PA
CBHW060810270326
41928CB00002B/44